The Stance To Lead
By Parker Bono

I dedicate this book to the American people and those who fight and fought for my right create this.

Chapter 1
Views

"If you put the federal government in charge of the Sahara Desert, in five years there'd be a shortage of sand." -Milton Friedman

---

The below statements are my personal views on an array of subjects at the federal level.

Immigration

- A virtual wall will be built consisting of drones, surveillance, and other barriers that will end the potential for illegal immigration and plans that will end the incentive of it.
- Illegals currently in country will have the opportunity of work visas and at most permanent residence but never citizenship. If people with Visas or permanent residence have police confrontations (that aren't minor) then they will have to leave (deported).
- Immigrants must learn English (fed. Gov. will pay)
- Children of illegal immigrants should not receive citizenship even if they were born here. (from here on out)
- Hire 10,000 more border patrol agents.
- Eliminate sanctuary cities. Laws on immigration to the U.S. should be obeyed throughout the U.S. with no exceptions.

Guns

- The Second Amendment is a right but the amount of bullets those guns could hold isn't. We should be allowed to own guns with a background check and a maximum bullet capacity per magazine should hold a maximum amount of 16 bullets and there should be further screenings for people who attempt to buy guns. People who attempt to buy a gun should have to take a mandatory psychological.
- The reason: 100 round clips are useless. This "Magazine Law" should be a national law as should further background checks/screenings/tests. Also, all instances of mass shootings are the result of crazy evil people with guns and a plethora of bullets.
- Eliminate "Gun Free Zones" in all of America.
- Allow concealed carry nationwide.

Foreign Policy

- Our military needs to be funded more. We have more growing threats from abroad and we need a strong military and that is something we currently lack.
- China and Russia have us beat right now both economically and militarily and we need more advanced technology rather than the same ideas. Our enemies become stronger and we become weaker.
- Foreign Terrorists should have no Constitutional rights.
- End the draft. If the war is worth fighting, people will volunteer.
- Continue to support our key ally Israel.

- Remain in NATO just make sure the other countries pay their fair share as we do.
  - Implementation of the URC
  - Attempt to make peace with North Korea.
  - The U.S. should formally declare war on ISIS.
- Everything going on in the Middle East is because of a lack of power. You can overthrow a dictator but it's not going to solve anything. We must first take away all power then redistribute it in a democratic way to help form and maintain democracy in Middle Eastern countries that need it the most.
  - Take out 50% of our troops located outside of the country.
  - Create many more military aircrafts, boats, and submarines.
- Don't allow syrian refugees. (If there are 100 cookies and two are poisoned, do you eat one?)

Education
  - We need to eliminate common core.
- Eliminate "Gun Free Zones" in schools (and have at least one armed official at each school)

Electoral
- ID required to vote to eliminate the possibility of voter fraud.
- Make election day a national holiday to ensure people have the time and opportunity to determine the future of their country.

- Make Election Day a National Holiday so it can be recognized for what it truly is, the most patriotic day of the year.
- Automatically register people to vote when you renew your driver's license.
- Campaign Finance Reform is wrong… "But to what extent can money buy power? Dismantling campaign finance laws can create more incentive for candidates to bend their will to the people who write the biggest checks. Yet money on its own clearly isn't enough to win a presidential race. Jeb Bush's super PAC raised more money in the first half of 2015 than President Obama's main super PAC did for the entire 2012 election cycle." -Forbes

Social
- Abortion should be illegal after 3 months.
- Continue to fund all aspects of Planned Parenthood other than abortion.
- Woman should make the same amount of money as a man if they have the same education or skill or experience as the man and companies should hire people as individuals.
- Government will support same sex marriage.
- Make smoking tobacco illegal since your stupidity shouldn't negatively affect someone else who didn't decide to smoke… AKA second hand smoke which kill over 55,000 each year, consisting mostly of children.

Environmental

- Global warming will continue to have many different views as to why it exists but it does exist. For this reason we as a country will try to "go green" not just for global warming but for health concerns.
  - Expand offshore oil drilling
- GMO products should be labeled as GMOs as should Organic products.
- Wind energy can still be used but we should no longer offer tax credits for it. We should also expand use of more efficient energy and use science to innovate currently existing technologies.

Economic

- Federal minimum wage should be raised from $7.25 to $10.00 gradually
- Physically and mentally capable people on welfare need to get a job and we need to help them get a job. (economical growth and unemployment rate will fall)
- Create more labor unions as they help the economy and are an efficient way for many to receive a job without needing special skills.
  - Flat income tax of 20%
  - Corporate income tax of 20%
- Social Security will be slowly eliminated. All people dependent on it, AKA who put money in will be given their current benefits and all people who haven't put money in won't need to but will need to put at least 3.5% of their income into a retirement fund that is not

Government run. Our goal will be to write laws on what you do to retire rather than forcing you to put money into Social Security your whole life. This system will allow businesses to compete for you and give Americans their own options for retirement and insure all people have enough money to have a good retirement and give individuals more money each year which will essentially help our economy.

- Create a maximum amount of time people can stay on welfare(1 year) so they have an incentive to get a job.
- People who deny a job should not receive welfare.

Domestic Policy

- Marijuana should be legalized but we need to crack down on the more deadly drugs, just take a different approach than the past failed war on drugs.
- There should be a term limit of 6 years for members of the House.
- People on "no-fly list" shouldn't be able to purchase a gun or ammunition.

Healthcare

- In order to attend public schools, students must receive certain vaccines.
- Some aspects of the Affordable care act need to be repealed while others need to be replaced. The middle class is paying money they can't afford and receiving nothing in return.

- Healthcare should go beyond just a state level and all healthcare companies should compete nationwide.
- We should stop offering all forms of subsidization for illegal immigrants.

Criminal

- Police officers must wear body cameras. This protects the officer and the victim since there is a definitive answer to all the questions we may have.
- Convicted felons who did their time should have the right to vote.
- Solitary confinement should be banned for people under the age of 16.

Science

- The United States must return to space and manned space travel missions should be government funded.
- Study space to develop technologies revolved around it.
- Increase fundings for science and therefore innovation.

Chapter 2
Economics

"In economics, the majority is always wrong." -John Galbraith

---

Since 1913, the year the Federal reserve was founded, the value of our currency has gone down over 90%. The Federal Reserve is the reason for our national debt. The Federal Reserve also benefits international bankers. The Federal Reserve will be eliminated and replaced with something else detailed in this plan.

They say that money doesn't grow on trees but actually, our current banking system creates currency faster than trees can grow. Also, our money is made of paper so it technically does. Most people don't understand our economy, yet alone how our currency is made/created, so i'll simplify it for you.

The system starts when political candidates say "Vote for me and i'll give you more stuff than my opponent will." But we know that nothing is life is free so this money has to come from somewhere. To fulfil their promise, the politicians spend more money than is available, and this is called deficit spending. To pay for this deficit spending, the U.S. Treasury borrows currency by issuing a bond. A bond, in case you didn't know, is basically an IOU. It's a piece of paper that promises to pay back the money you put in plus interest.

What many don't know is that these bonds are our national debt. These bonds are to be payed back by the next generation.

Therefore, when the government issues a bond, it is taking prosperity out of the future for a quick cash flow it can have today. The treasury then holds a bond auction where the world bank's show up to buy part of our national debt in the form of bonds, and then they get to make a profit off of it in the form of interest. The international banks always benefit from our system and that will stop. I will explain how it will stop after I am done explaining the process.

Then, through open market operations, the banks sell the bonds to the Federal Reserve for a profit. To pay for these bonds, the Federal Reserve uses their checkbook and writes checks from an account with a $0 balance on it. Now, if you or I did this, it would be called fraud, but I guess it's totally fine for the Federal Reserve to do it. To quote the Boston Federal Reserve: "When you or I write a check, there must be sufficient funds in our account to cover the check, but when the Federal Reserve writes a check there is no bank deposit on which that check is drawn. When the Federal Reserve writes a check, it is creating money." A check is also an IOU. A check basically says "Here is an IOU for this much cash, now all you have to do is go to the bank and pick it up." After the Federal Reserve gives their checks to the bank, currency springs into existence. The banks then take that currency and buy more bonds from the U.S. Treasury.

It's very important that you understand this whole process as it is key to understanding how it affects you and I.

To recap, the U.S. Treasury issues bonds, the banks buy those bonds with currency, the Federal Reserve write checks to the banks in exchange for the bonds, and currency is created. What's basically happening is that the Federal Reserve and the U.S. Treasury are just swapping checks and bonds, using the banks as middlemen, and evidently creating currency. This process continuously repeats, enriching the banks but indebting the public by rising the national debt. The final result is an excess of bonds at the Federal Reserve, and an excess of currency at the U.S. Treasury.

The next part of the system is when the U.S. Treasury deposits the new currency into different parts of the Government. The Government then does deficit spending by spending the money on public works, social programs, the military, etc. The Government employees then deposit their pay into the banks. This may be shocking but when you deposit your currency into the bank, you aren't actually depositing it into an account to be safely held or saved. Instead, you are loaning the bank your currency, and within legal limits, they can do with it basically whatever they want.

This is where the system gets crazy. This is where something called Fractional Reserve Lending comes into play. Fractional Reserve Lending is the fact that Banks are allowed to reserve (or save) only a fraction of your deposit, and loan the rest out. Rates vary but for simplicity, I will use a 10% rate. If you make a $100 deposit into your account, in this scenario, the bank could take $90 of it and loan it out without letting you know. The bank must hold the $10 (10%) that you deposited, in case you want some. The $10 that actually got deposited is called vault cash. You may ask why your receipt says you have a $100 balance if the bank stole $90 of it and the answer is because the bank left an IOU called bank credit there in it's place. This may sound crazy, so here is a direct quote from the Federal Reserve Bank of New York, "Commercial banks create checkbook money whenever they grant a loan, simply by adding new deposit dollars in accounts on their books in exchange for a borrower's IOU" These are nothing but numbers typed into the bank's computers. And even though these numbers are very different from actual cash or currency since they only exist on a computer, they are still currency. So now, from your $100 deposit, there is now $190 in existence. Now, the only reason people take back loans from the banks is when they are going to buy something. So, the $90 that got loaned out will get spent by the borrower on something and the money will go to the seller. But then the seller deposits money into his bank account, and his bank loans out 90% of that, or $81 out to someone else, and leaves bank credit numbers in it's place. SO now there is $271 in existence. This process continuously repeats until a deposit of just

$100 can create up to $1,000 in bank credit, all backed by $100 in vault cash, or just 10%. In other words, your $100 deposit sprung $900 into existence. But as I said, ratios vary from 0% to 10% to 20%, and so on. The result is that the currency expansion is far greater than even this example makes you believe.

To recap, when currency is deposited into the banks, the banks can lend it out, and then it gets re-deposited and relent over and over again creating bank credit each time. This is where the majority of our currency supply comes from. In fact, it is estimated that 92%-96% of all currency in the U.S. is created not by the Government but by the banking system.

Lots of currency getting put into society may sound like a good idea at first until you realize that the prices of everyday goods and services act as a sponge on an expanding currency supply. The more currency that we have, the more things will cost. This is called inflation. The definition of inflation is an expansion of the currency supply. Rising prices are simply a symptom of inflation. So basically our entire currency supply is nothing but a couple of bucks put into the scam where the Federal Reserve and the U.S. Treasury swap IOUs and a bunch of numbers banks type into their computers. And as crazy as that sounded, this part is even crazier. We the people work for a portion of that currency supply. True wealth is your time but we trade away tens of thousands of hours for numbers that somebody printed on pieces of paper or typed into their computer. Now these numbers represent our blood sweat and tears. We the people are what give the currency its value. But here comes the craziest part. We work hard so we can save some of that currency so we can pay the tax collectors or the IRS. The IRS then gives that money to the U.S. Treasury so that way they can pay the principal plus interest on the bond that the Federal Reserve bought with a check drawn on an account with a balance of $0. Yes that;s right, much of our taxes don't go to schools or public services but to pay interest on the bonds that the Federal Reserve bought with a check drawn from an account that has nothing in it. As i stated previously, the Federal Reserve is committing fraud. But here is a very unknown secret. Before the implementation of the Federal Reserve in 1913, there was no need for a personal income tax. In 1913, the Federal Reserve was founded. That same year, the Constitution was amended to allow income tax. Do you really think that this was a coincidence? Just think of how much income tax you have payed in your lifetime. Then think of the amount of that that was silently transferred into the hands of those who own the system. Yes, this system has owners, and who they are is an even bigger secret I will address next.

But first, you need to understand the lie of the debt ceiling. The debt ceiling is based on a paradox. There was interest due on that bond, and there was interest due on every one of those loans that the banks made. This means that there is interest due on every single dollar that is in existence. Let me ask you something: If you borrow the very first dollar into existence, and that's the only dollar that exists in the U.S., but you promise to pay it back plus another dollar worth of existence, where do you get the other dollar from? The answer is you have to borrow that one into existence and promise to pay it back as well. So now there are two dollars in existence but you owe 4 dollars. (This process continues indefinitely and the result is there is never enough currency left to pay off the debt. This of course is excluding the assets the U.S. owns that are key in my plan to end the National Debt that will be achieved over an 8 year period) Therefore, the whole system is impossible.It is finite and it will come to an end one day even if we never got rid of the Federal Reserve.

The founding fathers of the United States knew about the dangers of central banking and fought to free themselves from this very thing. The Revolutionary War started off as a tax revolt. But now we must pay tax just to have a monetary system. After they suffered from the hyperinflation of the Continental Dollar that was printed in excess just fund the Revolutionary War, they understood the dangers of fiat currency. So to protect future generations from theft and out of control government, they wrote into the Constitution that "{No State shall} make any Thing but gold and silver Coin a Tender in Payment of Debts." They did this for the simple fact that you can't print gold and silver. Our current system isn't just unconstitutional but also robs us of what our founding fathers fought and died for. We all feel the effects of neglecting the Constitution right now. By forcing more currency into circulation, our purchasing power plummets. Inflation is a slow tax that is simply the result of this monetary system.

This system benefits those who create the currency and receive it first as they get to spend it into circulation before it has an effect on the economy. They are stealing purchasing power from you and giving it to the banks and the government every day. It's not like the people at the top don't know this. To quote the Federal Reserve, "The decrease in purchasing power incurred by holders of money due to inflation imparts gains to the issuers of the money." This whole system is fraudulent. Our whole system is nothing but a system of legalized theft.

This is the biggest con of it all. The Federal Reserve is not entirely federal. It has stockholders. There is no federal agency that has stockholders. A share of stock represents a percentage of ownership in an organization. This means that those shareholders are the owners of this organization. This makes the Federal Reserve a private corporation with owners. We know that the Federal Reserve has stockholders because if you go the the Federal Reserve's website, you will see that it states the stockholders receive an annual dividend of 6 percent. We know that in the beginning, these shareholders were the largest banks in the United States but due to company mergers and acquisitions throughout the years, we don't actually know who these shareholders are. I would assume that the owners are the banks that make a profit by selling part of our national debt in the forms of bonds to Federal Reserve who buys them with a check from nothing.

This system funnels wealth from working Americans to the government and the banks. It is the pure cause of the artificial good times and bad times of modern economies. This system is also only possible because we use currency, not real money like gold and silver as the Constitution states we shall. But worst of all, it is a form of enslavement. Nobody asked you if you wanted to pay tax today for the prosperity that we enjoyed throughout the last century. To quote George Washington, "No generation has the right to contract debts greater than can be paid off during the course of their own existence." By stealing prosperity of tomorrow for purposes today, we enslave ourselves and future generations.This all sounds very bad but there is hope. You are the greatest threat to this system. If you load and cock the gun, I will aim and shoot it. When I am elected President, I will fix it. I will fix this system by…

- Achieving 0% Unemployment
- Auditing and ending the Federal Reserve

- Promoting small business
- Giving a 0.000002% Tax Deduction per employee a company hires.
- Infrastructure growth and development
- Forcing the unemployed to volunteer
- Reforming welfare and immigration
- Import Tax
- Offer 1% tax deductions for companies that make products in the U.S.A.
- Offer 1% tax deductions for companies that hire

Plan	How many jobs we have lost since 2008	How many jobs we would gain in 8 years
Lowering Corporate Income Tax	2,500,000	3,000,000
Tax credit for made in U.S.A. items	0	1,000,000
Offering tax credits for each worker a company hires	0	1,000,000

Promoting small businesses and innovation	2,000,000	2,000,000
Offering incentives for companies and workers who hire or are hired to ecommerce jobs	1,000,000	7,000,000
True Immigration Reform	16,000,000	7,000,000

Below is my tax plan.

Current Federal Tax Rate	Future Federal Tax Rate
10%-39.6%	20%

Future Corporate Tax Rate	Current Corporate Tax Rate	Corporation Annual Income
10%	15%-39%	Under $400,000
20%	35%-38%	Above $400,000

Total Non-Federal Tax Rate	Future State Tax Rates	Future Local Tax Rates	Current State Tax Rates	Current Local Tax Rates
No More Than 7.5%	No More Than 5%	No More Than 2.5%	0%-7.5%	0%-5%

<u>No American Can Be Taxed More Than 27.5%!</u>
(Including Federal, State, And Local Taxes)

This Tax Plan is the simplest our nation has ever seen and will give the American people, particularly the middle class, great amounts of tax cuts, and will therefore give our economy tremendous growth.

Below is the future federal budget I would enact as President

NAT SPENDING (WITH NAT DEBT INCLUDED)
SOURCES OF INCOME (Annually)...
Corporate Tax(20%)- 400 Billion
Income Tax(15% Flat Tax)- 2 Trillion
Payroll Taxes(Same rate)- 1 Trillion
Other Taxes- 300 Billion
TOTAL: 3.8 Trillion

SPENDING
Social Security, Unemployment, And Labor- 1.3 Trillion
Health- 1 Trillion
Military- 550 Billion
Veterans Affairs- 150 Billion
Interest- 250 Billion
Education, Training, Employment, And Social Services- 100 Billion
Science- 50 Billion
Transportation- 100 Billion
Other- 175 Billion
TOTAL: 3.65 Trillion
125 Billion Surplus Each Year (Excluding Debt Plan)
AFTER 8 YEARS: 1 Trillion

Below is my plan to end the National Debt. All sources of revenue under these bullet points will be directed towards the National Debt.

I will...

- Raise All Excise Taxes 20% (10% Goes To 12%) *75 Billion Annually*
- Eliminate Loopholes And Some Credits *225 Billion Annually*
- Increase Tax Rate For Medicare Hospital Insurance By 1% *100 Billion Annually*
- Raise Federal Cigarette Tax Rate By $5 Per Pack *50 Billion Annually*
- 20% Tax On All Imports *500 Billion Annually*
- End War On Drugs *25 Billion Annually*
- Drill For Oil In The Green River Formation (Drill 5% Of Total Oil There Annually) *1.35 Trillion Annually (In Profit)*
- Legalize And Tax Marijuana And Online Gambling *50 Billion Annually*

EACH YEAR= 2.5 Trillion off of debt (Includes surplus from budget)

AFTER 8 YEARS: Surplus/elimination of national debt

This is my plan to save the middle class.

The middle class is currently being destroyed. The upper class is paying small amounts of money that they can easily afford. The lower class is receiving money from both the middle and the upper class for basically doing nothing and the middle class is paying money they can't afford. Middle class American's don't have access to what upper or lower class americans have access to. This puts the middle class at a huge disadvantage. My plan would change that.

Goals of the Middle Class Plan:
- Raise wages and increase the annual income for middle class americans
- Give the middle class more opportunities
- Don't make the middle class pay for things they can't afford
- Create more good jobs that pay well
- Eliminate wage theft that happens to 20% of men and 30% women.

How it will be achieved:
- Raising the minimum wage will definitely help middle class americans since they will be paid more as well. Also, by eliminating social security, Americans will make 6.5% more every year.
- One way to give the middle class more opportunities is to open up many corporate jobs that would pay

well. Millions of these jobs will be available since many companies will be returning to the U.S.

- The middle class can no longer afford to pay as much as they do. This is why there should be a flat income tax of 20%, with exceptions to the lower class. This would be fair to the middle class and allow them to earn more money each year. Also, if there was a maximum amount Americans could be taxed, that would help ensure that there is no chance that the middle class is taken advantage of yet again.
- If Americans wanted good paying jobs, the best solution would be unions. If Americans had the freedom to create and join unions as they wanted, well paying jobs would increase and the middle class would benefit.
- We should also eliminate wage theft. It happens far too often and it is wrong. It happens to 20% of men and 30% of women and it happens even more to people of color. If it was totally eliminated, everyone would receive more money.

Effects:
- Middle class Americans would make more money.
- Middle class Americans would receive better jobs.
- Middle class Americans would pay less in taxes each year.
- More unions would be created, so the economy would improve drastically.

- Wage theft would be eliminated so all Americans would no longer be wrongfully robbed of their well deserved money.
- The middle class would thrive once again, as it should!

Below will be the future trade policy in our nation.

Goals Of Trade Plan
- Bring China to the bargaining table
- Reclaim millions of American's jobs
- Strengthen our negotiation position
- Make companies come back to America.
- Make money rather than lose money every year on trade with China, as well as the rest of the world

How It Will Be Achieved:
- Declare China a currency manipulator.
- End China's Intellectual Property Violations which costs us $300 Billion and many jobs every year.
- Eliminate other countries unfair advantages.
- Tax countries 30% for all imported goods.
- Lower the corporate income tax to China's (30%) and make it a flat tax.
- Offer tax credits if you buy items or goods made in the U.S.
- End our National Debt and Deficit.

Effects:
- Companies would return to America
- Tens of millions of jobs would be available, making the U.S. a target for immigration (that would be done legally), and giving hope once again to the American Dream.

- The U.S. would make money on trade each year rather than lose money.
- China would finally get what it deserves for being corrupt for the last 20 years.

This is my plan regarding jobs and job growth in our nation.

Supposedly, about 6% of Americans are unemployed. I don't necessarily believe this number but we can still use it even though many of those people who aren't considered unemployed solely gave up looking for a job or were offered one but declined or were laid off or possibly even getting their money from extreme forms of welfare. Regardless, that number should still be far under 6% and it will if we follow this plan as designed… We need Jobs, an increased GDP, and a booming economy and we need it now!

Goals of the Jobs Plan:
- To lower unemployment rate to less than 1% by the end of two terms
- Create over 20 Million jobs by the end of two terms
- Lower inflation rates
- Raise GDP (Gross Domestic Product) by 50% or more
- Raise net worth of family earnings by 30% or more
- Lower interest rates
- Bring U.S. markets to all time highs and prove to Americans it is beneficial to save and invest
- Lower taxes to compete/match China
- Bring companies to the U.S.

How this will happen:

- Flat Corporate Income Tax and Income Tax of 20% (with exceptions to very small or poor people). This system will be modeled after China and will allow us to compete with China. Also stop taxing capital gains.
  - Create a "Reverse Inversion" (reversion is when companies leave the U.S.). With the 20% Corporate Income Tax.
- Our next goal will be to make companies bring their estimated $2 Trillion parked offshore back home as well. We will do this by just taxing that by 10% when they come back (one time). This would result in the government receiving $200 Billion in taxes and allow $1.8 Trillion to go into the economy.
  - Thirdly, we are going to want to make sure people buy the products made in the U.S. We will do this by giving tax credits to people when they buy products that are U.S. made.
  - After we secure the border, we will offer many temporary visas, or in many cases permanent residence but NEVER citizenship. They give up their right to vote when they come here illegally. Many people that come here demand a job and food stamps and when we give them that and they don't have to pay taxes, our economy falls.
  - Increase reserve requirements on the amount of money banks are legally required to keep on hand to cover withdraws. The more money banks are required to hold back, the less they have to lend to consumers.

If they have less to lend, consumers will borrow less, which will decrease spending.

Chapter 3
Security

"There are some who've forgotten why we have a military.
It's not to promote war, it's to be prepared for peace"
-Ronald Reagan

These are my goals regarding foreign policy.

As our relations with other countries changes drastically, Foreign Policy is a key factor to look at. We must find a way to be the greatest country in the world and have the greatest military in the world and ensure safety to our homeland and our allies. We must also ensure that countries like China pay their fair share. Some of our current enemies should also begin to become neutral or friendly, if possible-otherwise impose so many sanctions that the country is forced to comply. We can prosper, be the best, and we can create peace and we will under this plan!

Goals of the Foreign Policy Plan:
- To create peace
- To show power
- To protect in exchange for protection
- To defeat ISIS
- Stop patrolling the world

- Ensure that admission into the greatest country is exclusive to the greatest people who would like to immigrate here.

How it will happen:

- Negotiate and speak with other countries and prove it's beneficial to be allies or neutral rather than enemies.
- Fund our military more.
- Make members of NATO pay their fair share.
- Do many more airstrikes and put a small amount of highly skilled members of the military to defeat ISIS and have them come out every 6 months and send a new group of 250 in.
- Take back half of military members stationed outside of the U.S.
- Create a queue that applies when trying to immigrate to the U.S.

Effects:

- Relations with countries would improve.
- Our military will be the strongest in the world.
- We will be the most powerful country in the world.
- NATO members would do as they should.
- ISIS as we know it would be eliminated within 4 years.
- We would have half as many troops deployed overseas.
- A queue system would be applied to the immigration process.

This is a plan to ensure safety is given to all Americans.

Safety should be insured to all americans, no matter the location or ethnicity or place or time.This however is something that we currently lack as many Americans don't feel safe, many Americans are not safe, and many children are forced to grow up feeling just as scared as things as their parents are. Under my plan, every American would be able to feel safe in their own homes or at any public place.

Goals of the Safety Plan:
- To ensure safety is provided to all Americans
- To bring terrorism to an all time low
- To bring death to an all time low
- To ensure relations between Americans is at an all time high.
- To ensure all Americans are safe and feel safe.

How it will happen:
- People who could possess a threat will be punished and caught. We will make sure people are willing to speak up. People will start talking and stop doing terrible crimes.
- We will create a more sophisticated background check system. This would allow the good to come and the bad to leave. We will also survey areas all across america to ensure there are no chances of anything occurring. We will also have one armed person at

every public place. These guns will always be supplied by the government and in some instances, the people with them will be supplied by the government as well.

- Death, that is typically gang related, will be dealt with. We will break up gangs.
- Many americans don't trust each other, for obvious- but wrong reasons. This would stop as we would prove that it is safe and beneficial to be friendly and trust each other.
- Many Americans don't feel safe. For all the reasons listed above and many more, they will begin to feel safe again and they will be kept safe.

Effects:
- Americans would be guaranteed safety.
- Terrorism in the U.S. would fall.
- Death- typically gang related- will be dealt with, as will gangs in general.
- Relations among Americans would reach an all time high.
- Safety will be restored to all Americans.

Chapter 4
Health

"If you like your doctor or healthcare plan, you can keep it."
-Barack Obama

This quote was a blatant lie as premiums rose on average over 50%, thousands of doctors quit, many people had to change their plans and go to the Obamacare Bronze plan where you can't even get a percocet, and the middle class was once again penalized for trying to live. Below is my healthcare plan.

Welfare recipients should receive a form of healthcare that in case of an emergency, will cover them. This however would only last one year (6 months while they search for a job and 6 months while they earn money from a job.)

My healthcare plan would...
1. Repeal some parts of Obamacare and rewrite some other parts.
2. Remove the individual mandate.
3. Break away state barriers on health care providers.
4. Make health care savings accounts tax free and encourage use of them.
5. Make Medicaid a state level issue, not a Federal. Cut federal funding in half.

6. Allow oversea drug imports. This will drastically decrease prices.

Below is my plan for the future of Social Security.

Social Security, the term used to described a flawed system that has been stealing from Americans for generations. All Social Security is is an inter-generational transfer of wealth-and this transfer effects the next generation more and more every time. It's time to end the flawed system that gives out more money than it can afford to give and give Americans and other companies more opportunities. Americans will get what they deserve in my plan!

Basically, we are going to end social security and write new laws about retirement funds. Kind of like the Affordable Care Act, we won't present another government run retirement program rather laws for currently existing and future ones. Firstly, eliminating Social Security would give Americans about 6.5% more of their income each year. Then, our new laws will require Americans to put a minimum of 3.5% of their income into a retirement fund. Assuming you make the current average salary in America ($55,775) and invest the minimum (3.5%) into a retirement account, you would have about $600,000 in savings when you retire (at age 67) and if you live to the average life expectancy (age 79) then you would collect about $50,000 each year in pensions during your retirement or $4,150 a month. This assumes the average inflation rate of 3%. Instead, if you made that same annual income each year, and paid it into Social Security, your monthly pension payment would be about $2,500. This also equates in 3% annual inflation. The new law would provide the average American with $2,000 more each month as opposed to Social Security pensions with the same annual income, starting age, retirement age, and inflation rate yet you are taxed 3% more... and the government still finds a way to spend more than they have on this program.

The problem is this can't all happen over night. If it did, very bad things would happen although it would be beneficial in the long run. Instead, we will take everyone who hasn't put money into Social Security off of it as well as people born in the future. The situation for the already retried and people who have already put money in will remain the same until they die. Future adult workers will have to pay at least 3.5% of their income into a retirement savings account and future generations will have a much more prosperous retirement.

Chapter 5
Domestic Plans

"The Constitution only guarantees the American people the right to pursue happiness. You have to catch it yourself."
-Benjamin Franklin

This is my plan regarding the reformation of the welfare system.

About 1 out of every 3 Americans are on some form of welfare. Many of these Americans may need help, but what we are offering isn't efficient. We give enough money out each year in welfare programs to bring each person on welfare 4 times above the poverty line but because of misuse of the funds, many programs are wasteful. It's time for Reformation! Also, many people are dependent on free stuff welfare offers rather than going out and doing something. The current welfare system encourages dependence and costs the middle class far too much!

"Taxpayers today are paying the poorest people in America a trillion dollars a year not to work. And so that is what they are doing in response. In 1960, nearly two-thirds of U.S. households in the lowest-income one-fifth of the population were headed by persons who worked. But after the War on Poverty began in 1965, by 1991 this work effort had declined by about 50 percent, with only one-third of household heads

in the bottom 20 percent in income working at all, and only 11 percent working full-time, year-round. One central reason for the inequality between the top 20% and the bottom 20% is that according to the Census Bureau families in the top 20% work 16 times as much as families in the bottom 20%."
-Forbes.com- 2016.

I will...
- CAP WELFARE SPENDING AT $200 BILLION ((FEDERAL))
- ($250 BILLION SAVED EACH YEAR)
- MAKE ALL FORMS OF WELFARE HAVE A ONE YEAR MAXIMUM
- ELIMINATE CORPORATE WELFARE!

These plans will save each taxpayer about $1,500.

Welfare plans that will be eliminated (with current cost per year)
1. Lifeline, AKA Obamaphone-3B
2. LIHEAP-5B
3. WIC-10B

Many others that would add up to about another 38B.
Welfare plans we will lower spendings for (with current cost per year)
1. Child Nutrition- From 25B to 20B
2. EITC- From 85B to 75B
3. SNAP- From 80B to 50B
4. HUD- From 50B to 40B

5. SSI- From 56B to 30B

6. Medicaid- From 500B to 400B

Many others that will be addressed in per category plan...
Welfare plans we will expand (with future and current cost per year)

1. Pell Grants- From 35B to 50B

2. TANF- From 16B to 50B

3. Head Start- From 10B to 20B

4. Job Training- From 6B to 50B

If we do this and the other things that are addressed in the per category plan, our future will have many opportunities to do much better than we currently are doing.

Below is my per sector welfare plan regarding funding.

Category	Current Spending (In Billions)	Future Spending (In Billions)	Total Change (In Billions)
Cash	200	125	-75
Medical	600	500	-100
Food	100	75	-25
Housing	50	75	+25

Energy	5	5	0
Education	40	75	+35
Training	10	50	+40
Services	15	15	0
Child Care	20	30	+10
Community Developmen t	10	15	+5
Other	100	25	-75

We will also make all welfare Insurance recipients as well as welfare payment recipients who are unemployed volunteer until they find a job and they can only stay on welfare for one year. This way they earn job experience and contribute to the economy so in a way, they are earning the money.

Final: Save 200 Billion each year from taxpayers that pay into welfare and expand forms of welfare that have the greatest chances of creating success for families and individuals in the future.
"PEOPLE ON WELFARE WILL BE ENCOURAGED TO WORK, TRAINED TO WORK, AND THEY WILL WORK. CHILDREN WILL BE TREATED WITH IMMENSE RESPECT AND WILL HAVE A GREAT OPPORTUNITY TO BE A PART OF GREATNESS THAT RESIDES WITHIN

OUR GREAT COUNTRY AND THE AMERICAN DREAM!
ALSO, OUR MIDDLE CLASS AMERICANS WILL NO
LONGER SUFFER TO PAY FOR SOMEONE ELSE TO
SUFFER EVEN MORE WHILE ON WELFARE!"

Below are future policies regarding immigration.

Every year, millions of people from all over the world, but mainly Mexico, immigrate to the United States of America illegally. The result is the fact that many American's jobs are being taken away, drugs and crime coming through to the U.S. at rate that is definitely noticeable, and people who don't pay taxes yet still receive tens of billions of dollars in free education benefits, free healthcare benefits, free housing benefits, and free food stamp benefits, which costs Americans even more money. These results are not beneficial to America and therefore illegal immigration needs to come to an end and legal immigration needs to come to a new high. Immigrants who pay taxes like every other American citizen do indeed help our economy so we should let them come in legally just make sure they would be great enough for the greatest country in the world. We would do this by hiring more workers and doing far more sophisticated background checks but making it so those background checks are done quicker so people aren't stuck on the waiting list for years.

The current immigration system allows the following to happen: drugs to pour through, illegal immigrants to be housed in our prisons, a violent drug war to exist, gang violence to be brought to the U.S., and loss of jobs that could be given to unemployed Americans. All of these catastrophes can be prevented if we follow all of the ideas listed below. We will give higher rankings in the queue for immigrants who pass the background check and can prove they are able to do skill required jobs. This would make the unemployment rate fall, allow them to make money, and allow the government to make more money! This queue system would also help our economy. We should also defund sanctuary cities. U.S. immigration laws should be followed throughout the U.S. without exceptions. We should also increase punishments for overstaying a Visa. We should deport all criminal aliens currently in our prisons being funded by our taxpayers. We will give out permanent residency and visas to certain families and deport others, depending on the situation. We need to build a virtual wall since that is the most efficient method. This virtual wall would consist of sophisticated monitorization technology, including drones. We also will hire more border patrol agents, which will create jobs, and monitor more heavily other ways illegal immigrants come into our country such as through planes. Many other countries have walls to help stop illegal immigration from occurring. This number actually adds up to 35% of the countries in the world (65 to be exact) that have border walls, and the U.S. would be the 66th. We should also create a nationwide e-verify system, which would protect jobs for all unemployed americans. Finally, we should end birthright citizenship which is the largest magnet for illegal immigration. You should not be granted citizenship for being the child of an illegal immigrant, even if you were born here. That may sound wrong but it really isn't. In 85% of the world, birthright citizenship is illegal. If we do this, our country and it's economy would improve drastically!

This is a plan regarding the future of the FDA.

People are going to question why I am going after the FDA and to that I will question why the FDA is going after us by allowing dangerous ingredients to be put in our foods, being a very corrupt administration, and regulating over 20% of our economy. The FDA typically has a straightforward answer to drugs: make sure it is safe and effective if it is to be legal. It is essential that we continue to have monitorization of foods and chemicals and conduct studies that show side effects. This however isn't done well with the FDA. This, along with many other reasons, is why we must reform the FDa... and here's how to do it.

The process for approving new drugs in the U.S. takes a long time and costs a lot of money. But in trying to speed things up too much, Congress runs the risk of allowing drugs to reach the market that aren't necessarily safe. This will no longer be allowed. The FDA will not allow the use of any food or drug that has not passed their studies. We also will immediately recall an item if it begins to go under FDA investigation.

We all want our products to be safe but the FDA spends so much time trying to prove products are clinically useful which should be the job of patients and doctors. We will make it faster for drug companies to get approval by cutting the target review time of 10 months to five months which would also make drugs less expensive. Now Grandma and Grandpa don't need to spend over 10% of their Social Security check on drugs. Also, more breakthroughs would be made and more options would be available because more companies would enter the drug market.

We will immediately stop the fluoridation of water and will conduct a non biased FDA study on it for the first time in U.S. history. Over 23 human studies and over 100 animal studies linked fluoride to brain damage. Fluoride is the only drug forced as mass medication of the population despite the fact that once fluoride is added to the water supply, there is no way of controlling the dose; it goes to everyone regardless of age, weight, health, need, or nutritional status. Tooth decay, AKA the only supposed reason we fluoridate our water, has been found to be going down at a faster rate in non fluoridated countries than fluoridated countries. It is estimated that 41% of U.S. children have some form of dental fluorosis caused by excess fluoride. Finally, only 1% of the fluoridated water is consumed by humans… 99% of the fluoridated water goes down the drain and into the environment. Assuming the FDA study on fluoride shows the same result as almost every study on fluoride, we will permanently stop poisoning our own citizens.

Drug prices are on an extreme rise. Most recently, EpiPen prices have been going up a very substantial amount. EpiPen could only raise prices because they had no competition in the marketplace. That's odd, given that epinephrine isn't patented and has been synthesized for well over a century. In Europe, there are multiple competitors to EpiPen, but in the United States, the FDA has prevented competitors from entering the market – and the biggest competitor to EpiPen, Adrenaclick, is barred from substitution for EpiPen in prescriptions. We will immediately allow free market competition for the EpiPen and will stop allowing lobbyists to control what is regulated or not by the FDA.

In the past, the FDA has done many horribly corrupt things. Just some consist of faked X-ray reports, forged retinal scans, phony lab tests, and secretly amputated limbs. These were all done by FDA scientists that figured they could get away with it. Most don't know about this because when the FDA finds scientific fraud or misconduct, the agency doesn't notify the public, the medical establishment, or even the scientific community that the results of a medical experiment are not to be trusted. On the contrary. For more than a decade, the FDA has shown a pattern of burying the details of misconduct. As a result, nobody ever finds out which data is bogus, which experiments are tainted, and which drugs might be on the market under false pretenses. The FDA has repeatedly hidden evidence of scientific fraud not just from the public, but also from its most trusted scientific advisers, even as they were deciding whether or not a new drug should be allowed on the market. We want the FDA to have much more freedom but only to an extent. We must simply implement policies that make sure this doesn't happen and punish the ones who did it if it is done.

The FDA has let some ingredients through that should have never been given to the public... You, your children, your parents, etc. My FDA commissioner will order the banning of the drugs listed below for reasons that are also listed below.

Ingredient	Reason It Should Be Banned
Olestra/Olean	blocks the body's ability to absorb essential minerals and vitamins.
Brominated Vegetable Oil (BVO)	Increases the risk of breast cancer, prostate cancer, ovary cancer, thyroid problems and cause death in children.
Potassium Bromate	linked to kidney problems, neurological disorder and cancer.
BHA/BHT	insomnia, increased appetite, loss of energy, liver and kidney damage, fetal abnormalities, mental and physical retardation, cancer and baldness.
Azodicarbonamide	asthma and allergies.
Artificial food coloring and synthetic food dyes	linked to neurological problems, brain cancer, ADD, ADHD and hyperactivity.
rBGH or rBST hormones	linked to breast and prostate cancer, thyroid

	disease, diabetes, obesity, infertility, asthma and allergies.
Neonicotinoid pesticides	linked to colony collapse of bees.
Arsenic	causes cancer or even death
Formaldehyde	can damage human cell and long term exposure to Formaldehyde can cause cancer including leukemia and short term exposure can cause watery or burning eyes, asthma, headaches, skin irritation, and nausea.
Potassium Bromate	causes cancer in the thyroids, kidneys and other body parts
GM Corn	severe stomach inflammation and enlargement of the uterus
GM Soybeans	allergies, sterility, and birth defects

Below is a my plan regarding the VA.

The current VA has allowed over 300,000 veterans to die waiting for care. This of course was wrongly excused. This must and will come to an end.

Goals of the Veterans Plan:
- Modernize the VA
- Insure that our veteran's invisible wounds are recognized and helped.
- Stop corruption and fraud that currently exists in the VA
- Ensure veterans have easy access to healthcare that would help them and their needs.

How it will be achieved:
- Fire the current VA executives.
- Increase funding for PTSD, traumatic brain injury, and suicide prevention so our veteran's and their invisible wounds are recognized.
- Create a plan that is affiliated with the VA that gives all veterans access to healthcare.
- Modernizing technology used in the VA.

Effects:
- Fraud would be eliminated from the VA after the firing of the current executives.

- The VA would be modernized. The Veterans Plan would make it happen by accelerating and expanding investments in state of the art technology to deliver best-in-class care quickly and effectively. All veterans should be able to conveniently schedule appointments, communicate with their doctors, and view accurate wait times with the push of a button.
- All veterans would have access to healthcare that is run by the VA.
  - The injuries associated with veterans would be recognized, diagnosed, and solved. This would drastically improve the health of our veterans.

This is my plan regarding criminals and the law.

Every year the failed war on drugs causes many people to be charged for drug use more harshly than murderers are charged. Also, many past felons still don't have the right to vote. They are americans and their voice matters just as much as ours. The death penalty should remain for certain cases and we should crack down on the more dangerous drugs but legalize recreational use of marijuana.

Goals of the Criminal Plan:
- To ensure all Americans get to use their right to vote.
- To ensure equality in sentencing.
- To enforce strict punishments for strict laws that were broken.
- To reform the war on drugs and instead work on rehabilitation more than punishment.

How it will be achieved:
- Laws would be changed to give past felons the right to vote.
- Sentences would have new requirements so stricter law breakers receive stricter punishments and smaller law breakers receive more minor punishments.
- Offer rehabilitation to drug and alcohol abuser, etc.

LEGALIZE RECREATIONAL USE OF MARIJUANA
^GOOD SOURCE OF TAX REVENUE^

Effects:
- No voting rights will be falsely taken away.
- People will be fairly charged and fairly punished.
- Strict and minor lawbreakers will receive strict and minor punishments.
- Less criminals will commit second offenses.
- People will no longer import marijuana (The #1 drug that comes illegally to the U.S.) illegally since they can go anywhere else rather than buy it illegally.

Chapter 6
Miscellaneous

"One of the penalties for refusing to participate in politics, is that you end up being governed by your inferiors." -Plato

---

This is a brief statement on my current view of our nation as well as what we must do to fix it.

"Although America is brainwashed, the spirit of America will never die!" -Parker, 2016

Right now, our country is at a turning point. We are facing problems in many ways and we need someone who is willing to identify those problems and do something about them. Here at home, we feel as though people deserve equal result rather than equal opportunity. All people deserve the same opportunity to succeed but what you do with it is up to you.

Extreme forms of welfare ensures people are stuck and dependent on welfare since i keep getting a small amount of stuff for free so I don't go out and do anything. Economically, we need to replace NAFTA and bring jobs home. We lost over 1,000,000 jobs to NAFTA and have lost far more to China. We treat small businesses terribly and larger corporations even worse. If we lowered our corporate income tax, companies may actually want to come back.

Right now, they have no incentive to stay! Our markets are fine but could and should be doing much better.

At the border, we are faced with a crisis. Illegal Immigrants are rewarded for coming here illegally, and the fact that they are even able to come here illegally in the first place says a lot. We could fix this by creating a virtual wall with drones, surveillance, and many other forms of innovative technology. Then there's the "Syrian Refugees". Here's a good analogy about them: Imagine there are 100 cookies but 2 are poisoned. Do you risk it and eat one? Roughly about 98% of the time, they are most likely good people but because of the fact we can't really vett them, all we can look at is the fact that there are some bad. Besides, they have many other places they can go and at this time we just can't afford to take any risks. I'd suggest us helping them go to another country but not admit any into our country. Saudi Arabia has over 100,000 tents with perfectly running water and electricity they can go to.

Guns have seemed to split America into a divisive two when there is a simple and logical answer to it all. Rather than ban a type of gun, how about we encourage gun ownership but at the same time enforce fool proof screenings/psychological tests. We can't just hand out guns and we shouldn't take away rights either. This way, America will be safer and both sides will be happier. We could also restrict the amount of bullets in guns as well to 16. This is solely to prevent the possible damage that could be done if our system fails and because 100 round clips are useless. We will also eliminate "Gun Free Zones" in all of America. This is because you don't need to write laws for good people and the bad people don't care about those laws. All these zones do is set up targets. We should eliminate gun free zones and have armed officials at all current gun free zones. This helps minimize or eliminate the damage potentially done.

One of the most detrimental programs called Social Security will be ended and replaced with laws about retirement. We simply can not continue Social Security as it is terrible on both sides. The government has to spend more on it rather than other programs that are far more beneficial and the people must pay more in taxes. It must change! Another detrimental policy called the Affordable Care Act will be repealed and replaced but not entirely. In the end, it will work out for everyone.

Here at home, he have some problems to. I believe that Marijuana should be legalized and taxed, as well as online gambling. This will only give the government more money and the people a better country. We will ensure that you are safe when you are anywhere in the country. Americans must and will feel safe in and out of their homes. The relationship between the people and our law enforcement needs to improve. We will help build trust by making police wear body cameras. Finally, our country will return to the moon and be far more involved in Science.

From another country's perspective, we are pretty weak. Russia and China and North Korea and Iran do many things that basically tease America and their message of "we're better than you" seems to be true when it isn't. I will do whatever is necessary to prove the rest of the world and Americans that we are the greatest, strongest, biggest, and best country in the entire world and you can't do these types of things to us and expect nothing to occur. China manipulates its currency while Russia expands their territory trying to make us take the bait in both Ukraine and in Syria while Iran is getting Billions of dollars from us and basic access to Nukes… they don't need us to survey their facilities because with the amount of money we gave them, they can buy their own nuclear weapons! This all happens while their government shouts "death to America" and North Korea threatens our allies.

Smaller countries or groups such as ISIS are taking control of the Middle East and we keep falling for the bait of other countries and our current flawed leaders would probably go to war in the Middle East… for the third time and most likely need to spend many lives, dollars, and time to basically get nothing. We can't do anything really that will work unless we do what I proposed: A small amount of highly skilled military members to be sent in as ground troops and take them out and replace them every 6 months. If we do this and continue airstrikes except at a higher rate, ISIS should be eliminated within two years and if we then take out the Iranian President, Syrian President, and restore territory and homes and a democracy to the Middle East, we should be able to re-stabilize the Middle East. Our nation will also continue support for Israel. Our "Free Trade" plans are nowhere near free trade and free enterprise. Instead, it's just other countries yet again taking advantage of America. And you may not hear about this one often but our allies are not paying their fair share. Japan, Canada, Italy, Turkey, France, Germany, Mexico, and other allies don't help as they should. We can not let it continue...

Below is my idea for a military partnership between Russia, the U.S., and China.

We will create an alliance between Russia, China, and the United States. These nations would fight and conquer whatever was diplomatically necessary. These nations, with their extreme military power, would aid us in fights against terrorism, and would be a good alliance.

This alliance would be for militaristic purposes only. It will cause all 3 nations to spend ⅓ of what they would have to if they conquered the subject on their own. The majority of the 3 nations must agree to the policy or plan if all 3 nations are to work together on it.

This alliance would last 10 years and may be renewed after expiration. The alliance will help us renew relationships and help the 3 superpowers remain superpowers rather than the 3 superpowers going against each other and causing the 3 nations and the world to suffer. Meetings will be held monthly between the 9 members of the URC council (3 will be appointed by each nation). 5 of the 9 members of the council must agree if the three nations are to perform the action being voted on. Every year the President's of each nation will meet. The location of the meeting will alternate each year (United States, China, or Russia). This relationship will be beneficial to all 3 nations as well as the world.

Below is a basic blueprint for what will happen in the first year of my administration.

My first year in office would consist of the most changes. These changes will reform America to our well deserving prosperous state. During my first year in the Oval Office, we will...

- Do all we can to end illegal immigration, with a very sophisticated system with expansion of 21st century technology
- Eliminate Sanctuary Cities (Day 1)
- All immigrants will learn English before being accepted into the U.S. (System/Law implemented Day 1)
- Eliminate our "First come first serve" border system and replace it with a totem poll. If you can contribute more to society, you will be admitted before someone who can't (System/Law implemented Day 1)
- Expansion of border patrol agents (10,000) (First Week)
- Deportation force (10,000 people) (1st Month)
- Give enough money to Flint, Michigan for them to fix the water crisis in a year (Day 1)
- Repeal and rewrite Affordable Care Act (Day 1)
- Place a maximum capacity on magazines (First Month)

- Have U.S. health experts create a psychological test for future gun buyers to take
- Allow concealed carry nationwide (First Month)
- Eliminate "Gun Free Zones" (First Month)
- Spend another $100 Billion on U.S. Military
- Eliminate Common Core Standards (1st Month)
- Meet with Kim Jong Un
- Have a meeting with both Putin and Xi Jinping at the same time (First 6 Months)
- Eliminate Social Security (for all who don't currently reap its benefits)
- Ban abortion after 3 months (First Month)
- Stop federally funding the abortion part of Planned Parenthood (Day 1)
- Move towards equal pay
- Make election day a national holiday (Day 1)
- Raise federal minimum wage to $10
- Get all physically and mentally capable people off welfare.
- Lower Corporate Income Tax to 20% (First Month)
- People who deny a job will not receive welfare (Law implemented Day 1)
- Legalize and tax online gambling and marijuana (1st Month)
- Term limit of 4 years for Congress (1st Month)
- People on "No-Fly List" can't buy gun (1st Month)
- Eliminate state lines for healthcare (Day 1)
- All law enforcement will need to wear body cameras

- Officially declare war with ISIS (First Month)
  - Much More Miscellaneous Items...

Below is what I believe and hope the future of America will look like after my election.

The future of America is at a tipping point. Assuming i'm elected to the presidency, a huge page will turn in our history that will give us prosperity and restore greatness to everyday Americans. Everyone will be awoken and we will be the #1 Global Superpower and every country in the world will know America is back and better than ever before!

If elected, our border will be secured futuristically. Illegal immigration will no longer be a threat and illegals currently in the country will be dealt with depending on the scenario but we will ensure that illegals are overall no longer a true issue. Our border force will be superior to all other countries as well as our border technology. At the border, America will be #1.

Another important issue is guns. Gun magazines will have a maximum capacity of 16. Concealed carry will not only be allowed nationwide but encouraged. All "Gun Free Zones" will be eliminated and an armed official will be placed at each one of these places. A psychological test will be made for future gun owners and overall, the very small threat of guns will be much much smaller and gun ownership will be encouraged.

Our foreign policy will be amazing. I will work together with so many other leaders of other countries and even ones that we don't work with. I will want to meet with Kim Jong Un, as well as Putin and Xi Jinping very quickly. Our military will be expanded extremely but we will withdraw from many places where we are not immediately threatened. In all non domestic bases, we will cut deployment in half. By the end of my first term, we will have two new airplanes, with a fleet of 200. We will have a new submarine with a fleet of 10. Also, a new navy ship with a fleet of 25 and a new helicopter with a fleet of 100. Our military will be so large we won't need to use it rather than so small we can't use it. We will formally declare war with ISIS and defeat them by the end of my first term. NATO will pay their fair share and we will remain a member. China will be put where it belongs on the totem pole and we will help refugees find refuge elsewhere such as in Saudi Arabia where they literally have 100,000 empty and vacant tents they could use equipped with full electricity but never house them here. As I have said many times, it's very risky and we can't take a risk right now. We will still help them but they have so many other places they could go for refuge and as we saw with Germany, it didn't really work out very well.

Economically, we will help promote business growth by lowering the corporate income tax to 20%. We will get people who are currently mentally and physically well off of welfare and if they deny a job, they will no longer receive welfare. We will put a limit on how long people can receive welfare with the exception of children related benefits. The fraudulent Social Security program will be eliminated. People who haven't put any money into Social Security won't need to deal with it and will never put a penny into it and people who have put money in will receive their promised pensions. The federal minimum wage will be raised to $10. We will lower tax rates on income brought over sea so we can get the $2 Trillion companies have offshore back here which would be beneficial to both parties. Our unemployment rate would go below 1%, our GDP will rise, and overall, economically, we will thrive and surpass China and all other countries in the economic world.

Here at home we will legalize and tax "sins" like marijuana and online gambling. Congress members will begin to have term limits of 4 years. The Affordable Care Act will be partially repealed and replaced. Law enforcement will need to wear body cameras to give definitive answers. We will return to space and get scientifically involved much more so our country can thrive and our movement will succeed.

Below are some very good quotes on an array of issues.

- "Coming here illegally doesn't make you any more of an immigrant than breaking into someone's house makes you part of their family."
  - "Being offended doesn't make you right."
- "Saying pistol grips make guns more dangerous is like saying race stripes make my prius go faster."
  - "If Kaepernick refuses to stand for the national anthem to protest racial inequality then will he refuse to take his paycheck to protest income inequality?"
  - "In 1776, our country's greatest leaders led us and they haven't been seen since."
- "Welfare's goal should be to end its existence, rather than expand its existence."
"The other day I saw a sign, it said "please don't feed the birds, feeding creates a dependent population. That is a potential health hazard and creates a costly mess and I asked why this logic isn't used in our society."
- "Ever wonder how the Federal Reserve works? Just look at rule #11 of Monopoly. It says "Some players think the bank is bankrupt if it ever runs out of money. The bank never goes bankrupt. To continue playing, use slips of paper to keep track of each player's banking transactions until the bank has enough paper

money to operate again. The banker may also issue
"new" money slips on slips of ordinary paper." That's
what the average person would call corrupt."

- "When you lie to the government, it's a felony but
when the government lies to you, it's called politics."
- "Good people don't need laws that tell them how they
should act and the bad people don't care about those
laws and the worst people of all, the politicians,
always find a way to write those laws."
- "Capitalism distributes unequal amounts of wealth
while socialism distributes an equal amount of
poverty."
- "If the Cigarette Tax is meant to stop people from
smoking than the Income Tax is meant to stop people
from working."

Here are just some of the many effects of my administration will have.

- Borders would be secure and the growing number of people who come here legally would drastically improve our economy.
- Mass shootings would drastically decrease and the ones that do exist wouldn't result in as many casualties.
- Our military would be far more technologically advanced than ever before.
- ISIS's locations in Iraq and Syria would disappear within 2 years, although we will keep using our system there for an additional 2 years since they most likely will return.
- We would stop policing the world as much as we do today.
- Common Core would be eliminated so more Billions of dollars will be available for states and the failed and wrong system will go away.
- The possibility of voter fraud would be eliminated entirely.
- The salary gap between men and women will fall drastically meaning theoretical equal wages would exist. (even though they are already basically equal)

- Greenhouse gas related health concerns would be basically eliminated and the U.S. would "go more green."
- Minimum wage workers would make more money.
- Many people will no longer need welfare and wouldn't be dependent on it.
- Americans would make about 10% more each year and they would pay less in taxes.
- Corporations would hire many more workers every year so economy grows and unemployment rate falls.
- Less people will be on drugs.
- Veterans would be taken care of more than they currently are.
- Americans that need it will receive temporary health insurance.
- Fatal shootings done by officers or directed towards officers would happen less often.
- The U.S. would return to space and learn and study it. This should benefit our lives in the near future.
- America's National Debt would be eliminated within 8 years. If we kept doing this after 8 years, other countries will have debt with us and we would receive trillions in a surplus.
- Much more prosperous proposals...

Chapter 7
Views

"Be sure to put your feet in the right place, then stand firm."
-Abraham Lincoln

Below are some of the views of I have in regards to certain subjects in the state of California

California has the opportunity to be the greatest state in America, and it should be. We have so much money but people that don't know how to spend it correctly. We have so many problems and people that don't know how to fix it. That's where I come along… and here's how we fix it.

Immigration

- It is estimated that about 6.5% of California's population consists of illegal immigrants. That's about 2.5 Million people! We will have an expansion of border patrol and have a fleet of drones that survey the border, monitor everything, and provide us evidence to use to help us find and catch them.
- The whopping 82 Sanctuary Cities in the state of California will no longer exist. Illegal Immigration is under federal jurisdiction but the federal government

doesn't mandate the fact that illegal immigration is under federal jurisdiction... and this is how sanctuary cities were created. The fact that they exist is troublesome and as we see in San Francisco and many other sanctuary cities, lives could be saved if they didn't exist. During my first day as governor, I will end sanctuary cities across California and stop funding them. More in "California Immigration Plan".

- We will focus mainly on the number of illegal immigrants currently in California and use a fleet of drone surveillance to help combat the new problems that we face at our border daily.
- Don't pay a penny to illegal immigrants which cost our citizens $25 Billion annually.

Economy

- Statewide minimum wage is currently $10. The average cost of living in California is currently $12.34 an hour. If we raised the minimum wage to $15, inflation would be crazy. If we incrementally raised the minimum wage to $12.50, people could afford to live in the Golden State and inflation wouldn't be drastic or detrimental to everyone else. This is a perfect Median to the extremely high $15 and the Extremely low $10.
- The current sales tax rate in California is 7.5% at the state level and a maximum of 2.5% at a local level. This will be changed to 6% at the state level and a maximum of 1.5% at a local level. This would allow the highest possible sales tax rate to be 7.5%.

- The current income tax in California varies from 1% to 13.3%. There are also a total of 9 tax brackets in California. We need simplification in this system. There will only be 4 tax brackets and a maximum tax rate of 10%. More info is located in my tax plan.
- California has the 14th highest unemployment rate, at 5.5%. We will bring this number down to 4% within 4 years.
  - We have some of the largest seaports in the world and they are the most secure ones to. We have the innovative Silicon Valley and the epicenter of bio-technology known as San Diego. Yet we can't figure a way to take advantage of this. We will...

Healthcare

- Rising rates, the detrimental costs for both people and the government, and lack of transparency are just some of the problems in California's healthcare system. This can and will be solved.

Education

- Change the mandated age for Kindergarten from 6 to 5. Notable studies show that if you start school at a younger age, you will have a far better life, far better results, more likely to take AP classes, etc.
  - Increase funding for K-12 schools by 16.5%. (state level)
  - We have the highest student to teacher, student to counselor, student to librarian, and student to administrator ratios in the country. This must and will

stop as we will hire another 200,000 teachers and administrators to public schools across the state.

- Innovate school technology and infrastructure.
- Fire all current "underprepared" or "novice" teachers who make up about 6% of California's teachers. Rehire new teachers who aren't incompetent at teaching the next generation.

Infrastructure

- We are going to fund the hell out of the infrastructure sector and we will increase the current $10 billion annual budget devoted to infrastructure to $60 billion each year. Were going to make sure this money isn't just getting thrown around either.
- Fix all current infrastructure that needs to be fixed within two terms as Governor.

Crime

- Expand "drug courts" in California. 49% of people who participated in drug courts repeated criminal activity as to 65% who didn't go to drug courts and repeated criminal activity.
- Quadruple the amount of camera monitoring/surveillance statewide.
- Deport criminals in our jails at once a well as illegal immigrants we end up catching in police confrontations. If they don't break the law or have contact with law enforcement, we won't go find them but if they do, bye bye.

- Ensure former offenders receive a job. Studies show prisoners who received a job within the first two months of being released had a far less chance of repeating criminal activities then those who were unemployed after the first two months.
  - More in "California Crime Reform".

Social

- Ban abortion statewide after 3 months.
- Legalize and tax marijuana statewide for recreational use and legalize and tax online gambling.
  - Make Election Day a statewide holiday.
  - Pass law that automatically registers you to vote when you renew your California driver's license.
    - Bring unemployment rate to under 3%

Drought

- This is a subject the current administration has no idea on how to handle. They are almost entirely to blame for the existence of the dreadful and detrimental California drought.
- It all starts with a total lack of rain, but it is important to recognize the fact that there is nothing we can do that will help this, even if the cause is "climate change". We can't produce more rain by spending more money and creating more regulations.
- Mandatory Drip Irrigation on all agricultural land. This would drastically help the drought as far more effective watering methods must be enacted and regulated.

- Offer $5 per square foot of land that is Xeriscaped in all of California.
- Open a Water Recycling plant in every California water district.
- Put water desalination in 10 major California cities (within two years). Those cities will be Los Angeles, San Diego, San Jose, San Francisco, Fresno, Sacramento, Long Beach, Oakland, Bakersfield, and Anaheim.

Guns

- Allow concealed carry statewide.
- Repeal the ban of "assault rifles".
- Hire 12,000 armed officials and put them into public schools in California.
- Create a psychological test gun owners and gun buyers need to pass to get a gun.
- The Second Amendment is your permit to own a gun, and it doesn't expire. In other words, end the need for a permit to have a gun.

Chapter 8
Economics

"The best investment you can make is in yourself" -Warren Buffett

---

Below are some economic policies I have in mind for the state of California.

California's economy is ranked 7th in the world. We have many people and many hard working people but the number of people who are unemployed is on the rise. Our labor participation rate is high and overall, our economy is fine, if not excellent but it can be better and it will be…

My goal of this plan is to mainly get people on the same page. Right now, most the people who are unemployed are unemployed since they don't have the skills needed to get the jobs that are being offered. We don't want this to continue so we will ensure high schools and community colleges are on the same page and ensure that graduates have the opportunity to succeed. We will also try to make sure that people who don't have a job, and especially those on welfare, start succeeding soon.

We will create a limit for how long a Californian can stay on welfare. This limit will be one year. We will also improve communications and training to ensure every welfare recipient will be trained to the level they need to get a job and if they decline the job, that's their fault. We will raise the minimum wage over time. It will eventually reach $12.50.

Simplification of our tax system will also help both parties. Only 4 tax brackets will be implemented and taxes will be lowered for most. Overall, our economy is fine but with these policies, our economy will flourish and our GDP should exceed that of France and maybe even the United Kingdom making our GDP the 5th highest in the world. These policies also support a lower unemployment rate and that number should be under 4% which would make our statewide unemployment rate the 10th lowest in the country. These policies would stimulate economic growth and must be followed if we want our economy to succeed.

Here is my proposed tax plan for the state of California.

Annual Income	Current Tax Rate	Future Tax Rate
Under $30,000	1-4%	2.5%
$30,000-$60,000	6-9.3%	5%
$60,000-$250,000	9.3%	8%
Over $250,000	9.3-12.3%	10%

I will eliminate all deductions and loopholes for the income tax so no one can essentially evade paying, no matter the circumstances.

Annual Corporate Income	Current Tax Rate	Future Tax Rate
Over $0	8.84%	5%

I will eliminate loopholes and deductions for the corporations as well. Far too many corporations get away with paying

Current Sales Tax	Future Sales Tax
7.5%	5%

I will pass a law that lowers the state level sales tax to 5% from the current and absurdly high 7.5%.

This is my proposed budget for the state of California

15 Billion from Corporate Income Tax
95 Billion from Income Tax
30 Billion from Sales Tax
10 Billion from License Tax
50 Billion from Special Funds
5 Billion from Marijuana and Online Gambling Tax
6 Billion from Other
General Fund: 216 Billion from 220 Billion

Pensions: 25 Billion from 40 Billion
Drought: 6 Billion from 0
Health Care: 20 Billion from 50 Billion
Education: 70 Billion from 60 Billion
Welfare: 10 Billion from 20 Billion
Transportation: 25 Billion from 10 Billion
Infrastructure: 30 Billion from 2.5 Billion
Government: 7.5 Billion from 7.5 Billion
Protection: 15 Billion from 15 Billion
Interest: 7.5 Billion from 7.5 Billion
Total: 216 Billion 210 Billion

Below is my plan to end the debt in California.

The answer to solving our $400 Billion statewide debt is actually very simple. All we need to do is have everyone over the age of 18 pay $2,500 annually for 8 years. The average income in California is $61,500 so on average, this will be a 4% tax. Our debt will be eliminated in 8 years. Then, we need to ensure our debt doesn't grow or redevelop. We will do this by mandating our spending and giving people a voice.

$2,500 is a simple solution but the mandating isn't. I've already addressed the fact that we will spend about $10 Billion each year on our interest alone regardless. If we don't try to eliminate the "wall of debt", that number will continue to rise detrimentally and eventually, we won't be able to recover without very serious problems. The $2,500 will bring in about $53 Billion each year. 100% of this will go to our debt. Our debt will be eliminated if we do this and stop overspending, and this is possible.

We stop overspending by simply being competent. We will allow the people to have a say. If we are going to spend a penny more than we have that fiscal year, the people will get a say and will have the opportunity to overturn and therefore make us rewrite the budget. This will give our representatives incentives to spend money how it should be spent. This is all so simple yet nobody has solved it... That stops today.

This is my plan to fix our infrastructure in California.

California has some very serious infrastructure problems that need to be solved in the very near future. These problems are caused by current and past administrations that don't know what the they're doing. I will fix these problems.

California's current representatives haven't addressed a very important issue: Infrastructure. They may address it but nobody has felt stronger on it then me. I think it is essential that our roads, bridges, tunnels, airports, schools, etc. remain in adequate condition and I believe we should expand in innovation. We should aspire to be great and our infrastructure should be the greatest in the country, rather than 34th.

It is estimated that we need about $20 Billion in infrastructure funding each year to fix our infrastructure problems within two terms as governor. Our public transportation is horrible and i'm sure we all remember the $100 Billion bullet train project that was disastrous, behind schedule, and won't work for a long time, and even when it is, it's insufficient. It's too late to fix any of that since construction is already underway and the money is already taken out of your pockets but it shouldn't have happened in the first place.

Anyways, in California, half of our dams our hazardous, 12% of our bridges are structurally deficient, there are $46 Billion in water infrastructure needs annually, $4 Billion needed for park funding, $20 Billion needed to fix our roads, $25 Billion needed to fix our schools, $1.5 Billion annually needed to fix our wastewater systems, and in order to fix it all in eight years, we would need at least $50 Billion each year. It can and will happen, here's how.

First, we will increase our current state budget devoted to Infrastructure. It is currently about $5 Billion and we will raise it to $31 Billion. We will also raise the current portion of the state budget devoted to public transportation from the current $9 Billion to $19 Billion. Specific spending listed below but basically we're going to fix what needs to be fixed and expand current projects and create new ones to innovate California.

ANNUAL BUDGET: $55 Billion
NEEDED TO BE FIXED: $440 Billion
YEARS TO FIX IT: 8

Type Of Infrastructure	Future Annual Spending	Years Needed To Fix
Aviation	$500 Million	8

Water	$6 Billion	8
Levees	$3.5 Billion	8
Ports	$1.5 Billion	8
Solid Waste	$10 Billion	8
Transportation	$25 Billion	8
Urban Runoff	$8.5 Billion	8
Wastewater	$5 Billion	8

We will begin to see incremental growth in our infrastructure if we follow this plan for the next 8 years and elect the only person who will implement this plan for the next 8 years (me).

Chapter 9
California Plans

"You have to think anyway, so why not think big?" -Donald Trump

---

The below plan is my plan for immigration reform in California.

Immigration in California is a very controversial topic but it shouldn't be. Illegal Immigration is very damaging to California and to the country and even it's people. Immigration should be encouraged but instead, with our current system, you're better off coming here illegally and receiving our benefits and housing we offer. We shouldn't reward criminals and their families and we no longer will...

California is a large state with a large amount of people, 40 million to be exact, but a number that isn't exact is the number of illegal immigrants currently in California. One thing however is certain and that is the fact that the number of illegal immigrants here in California is at least 2.5 million or 6.5% of our population. 70% of these illegal immigrants come from our neighbor: Mexico.

We need to first do as much as we can to stop more illegals from coming here. We will do that by using technological advancements, drones in particular as well as sensors that would help us develop a sophisticated monitoring system. The next step after this is to deal with the ones we have. The 2.5 million people who are illegal in California will be asked to step forward for evaluation. In order to pass the "evaluation", they will need to have no criminal record. The estimated 20% of illegal immigrants in California with a criminal record will not qualify for permanent residency and will therefore be deported. We will also have a drug test when they go through the "evaluation" Next, we have the educated. If they have a high school diploma, they can stay and if they don't, they need to get one if they want to stay. It is estimated that 40% of the illegal immigrant population in California has a high school diploma.

This leaves us with roughly 1 million currently illegal immigrants. If they would like to have permanent residency, they must pay taxes and the second they stop paying taxes or are criminally charged, they will be deported. Other than that, they're good to go and we will give them permanent residence. This will make them almost equal to you except for the fact they will be unable to vote.

Finally, we have Sanctuary Cities. They are terrible and have caused many deaths of innocent people. They are a magnet for illegal immigration and justify the crime and therefore, all 70 Sanctuary Cities in California should be eliminated. If we follow all of the policies listed in this plan, our border will stay advanced and safe, as will you and your family and law abiding currently illegal immigrants will have a path to permanent residency and the immigration system will be fixed.

This is my plan for the future of education in California.

Our children are being set back by government run education. We don't do anything to prevent or help this. K-12 schools aren't funded enough. 6% of our teachers are classified as "underprepared" or "novice" and must be laid off immediately. Our student to teacher ratio is extremely high and we must hire another 200,000 teachers who are capable of doing the job. We will take education out of Washington and we will fund education 16.5% more annually ($10 Billion) at the state level. If we don't do this and much much more, our K-12 education system will stay ranked 40th in the nation or maybe even lower.

About 83% of Californians believe our education system is problematic and I haven't heard a single efficient solution to the problem. About ⅓ of our state budget is spent on education and schools as well as school districts rely heavily on the money the state provides. Many of our students are in "reliance". 54% of them are on free or reduced lunch and 25% of them don't even speak fluent english, the language of our land.

Our student to teacher ratios are 26-1, much higher than the 15-1 state average. We will solve this problem by first hiring more teachers and faculty members, 200,000 to be exact. This would cut our ratio in half, making it 13-1. This would be beneficial to our future, AKA our children, to the schools and school districts, and to the government.

Next, about one in every 10 students in California will drop out of High School and another one in ten will not pass High School. That means one in every 5 students will not get a High School Diploma, something that is essential to success. We need to literally make this impossible and we will. We will make High School mandatory in California rather than allowing individuals to drop out when they turn 18. We will also allow children to be educated at a younger age making Kindergarten available to children aged 4 and older by the first day of school. We will also stop making schools gun free zones, as well as every other place in California. We will also make sure there is at least one armed official at each public school in California and this will prevent school shootings and lower the fatalities associated with them. If we follow all the plans listed above, our educational system will thrive!

This is my plan for healthcare in California.

California's Health Care problem is a lesser known issue but it effects everyone. 30% of people in California receive Medicaid or Medical benefits. Californians pay about $7,000 per person each year in healthcare services. These services amount to $75 Billion annually in the state budget alone which is about 37% of the state budget. We need reformation!

California has more people than any other state and therefore needs to have greater leadership than anywhere else in the country so we can take care of all of our people only at a far more affordable rate and when I say affordable, I'm not talking Obama affordable… I'm talking affordable for the people and the government, and this is possible.

Premiums are rising on average about 40% in California. Last year, 20% of Californians reported they didn't go to a doctor because of the price. Medical costs have doubled over the last 10 years and the state of our Healthcare system is disastrous and our elected representatives aren't committed to lowering these rates or the number of people on Medicaid. Instead, they simply put more and more money into a terrible system that needs to, and will be, fixed.

We will drastically defund Medicaid. It's extremely high $50 Billion annual cost will be lowered to a $20 Billion annual cost. We will no longer support reliance on welfare at any point in time. We then will reform the insurance regulations that are the pure cause of higher rates. Lack of transparency, lack of doctors, the raise of rates, and terrible financial management are the huge problems in California's Health Care system and they will all be solved if we follow this plan.

Below is my plan for crime reform in California.

Violent crime rates in California's 15 largest counties rose on average 10% in 2015 and rose about the same percent on a statewide level. Property crime also rose in those same counties an average of about 6% and about 5% on the state level last year. Overall, crime is on the rise... and it shouldn't be. Whoever commits these crimes, of any kind, whether they be misdemeanors, felonies, etc. should be punished and punished fairly. Our current judicial system punishes second time drug users more than rapists or murderers, which is wrong. We will fix the problems associated with our judicial system and we will also lower violent crime rates

One crime that is committed on a large scale level in California is illegal immigration. The vast majority of these illegals come from the neighboring country known as Mexico. It is estimated that about 7% of California's 40,000,000 residents are illegal. Despite only accounting for 7% of the population in the state of California, they account for 13% of the population in California's prisons. About 15,000 illegals are in our prisons and as governor, I will demand their deportation as well as their monitoring within my first week. It also doesn't help when all of the sanctuary cities in California rank in the top 20 for crime rates per 1,000 citizens. We will also have much higher security at our border to prevent further illegal immigration...if you would like to see my more in depth plan for this, go to my California Immigration page.

Crime isn't the only problem. The real problem is the amount of money we spend on these criminals. We spend about $10 Billion each year on prisoners or about $65,000 per inmate each year. We only spend about $10,000 per student each year. This means we put 6.5 times as much money into people who broke the law compared to people who are still learning the laws and attempting to be nothing like the prisoners. We will cut funding to prisoners and prisons and raise funding for our future. We will cut spending by 80% to prisoners. The new cost per prisoner will be about $13,000. This will make California the lowest cost per inmate state in the nation.

Illegal immigration isn't the only crime committed on a large scale in California. Property crime is extremely popular in California. 1 in 40 people in California commit property crime. This is about 2.5% of the population or about 1 Million cases each year. As Governor, I will double the minimum fees as well as sentences for property crimes such as petty theft, burglary, or vehicle theft.

We will totally reform sentencing in California. 90% of inmates in California have been there before and were returning. This is because California has absolutely horrible rehabilitation processes and programs. It's an epidemic in all of America. We are so worried about some guy getting caught with an ounce of Marijuana and we continue to try to criminalize it at such an extreme cost. This paves way for a black market. This also paves way for overdoses. I'm not pro total decriminalization, but I am pro efficiency… and this isn't efficient. We spend roughly $57 a second to fight drugs. The war on drugs has been a total failure and by definition, it is insanity… AKA, doing the same thing repeatedly but expecting a different result. We will no longer spend this vast amount of money to fight drugs and will invest our money in the right areas to ensure that California is made efficient as it was before.

These are my plans regarding guns in California.

Liberals have taken our great state over. I'm not saying conservativeness is the other way to go, i'm just saying liberals sure as hell aren't the right way to go. What we need is honesty. Taking away rights isn't going to help get guns away from people who will use them to cause harm. Good people don't need laws to tell them what to do and bad people don't care about the laws. They will always find a way to get a gun. The idea assualt weapons are bad is simply because of a great branding campaign. "Assault Weapons" accounted for 3% of murders over the last 5 years nationwide… 3 times as many murders were the results of hands and feet. Although it is true that assault weapons or more so semi automatic weapons do more damage when used, they are rarely used.

We will allow concealed carry without a permit. The Second Amendment is your permit to own a gun and that permit never expires. We however will ensure that the people who get these guns are non-violent and mentally stable. We will have a psychological test we will make each person who attempts to buy a gun go through.

We will repeal the ban on "assault weapons". Last year, our gun statistics showed that our "death by assault weapons" were the 10th highest by state in the country. We had 3.4 deaths by assault weapons per 100,000 people. Idaho has no regulation on assault weapons yet they had 0.8 deaths by assault weapons per 100,000 people. Also, California's statewide gun ownership is about 20% and Idaho's gun ownership is about 57%. It is like this in many other states as well and it proves we should encourage gun ownership in response to gun violence.

We will put over 12,000 armed officials in California public schools. These people will be a member of a union that is supported by the state. The people in this union will need to be trained and pass certain tests and the safety of your children will be ensured.

Overall, guns have been a very debatable topic yet the resolution is very simple. It is a fact that more guns equals more safety. Higher gun ownership equals lower gun murder rates. We should encourage gun ownership and make sure that those gun owners are suitable to own those guns. If we follow this plan, our gun violence rates will go down and we will be protected by more than a phone.

Below is my plan to end the current drought in California.

Unless you've been living under a rock, you are well aware of the fact that California is in a drought. Our current administration created this drought and is the reason it still exists. My plan will put an end to the drought and ensure efficiency and productivity when it comes to our water and our water systems.

We will start by evolving our irrigation technology. About 43 million acres are used for agriculture in California. The water management at these places are terrible. We will force all places used for agriculture to use drip irrigation. This will save us about 5 million gallons of water each year and not cost us a penny.

Next, we will use much more rain runoff systems. This is simple and cost effective. This will save California about 0.5 million acre feet of water each year. We will also offer $5 per square foot of land xeriscaped. Xeriscaping will save us about 1 million acre feet of water each year. Desalination plants will also be opened and used. We will install 5 of these each year, costing us about $2 Billion each year. This will save us about 0.5 million acre feet of water each year. What will help us the most is mandatory drip irrigation. With 21st century efficiency in our agricultural systems, we will save about 5 million acre feet of water each year. Since our current deficiency is about 6.5 million acre feet per year, or

2.2 Trillion gallons of water each year. We will begin to have a surplus within 4 years with innovative technology and we will once and for all end our water deficiency.

This doesn't mean the drought is fixed, it just means we will be able to save more water to help contribute to end that drought. To end the drought within 4 years, we must do many different things and we must do them efficiently and effectively. Right now, we need to get about 11 trillion gallons of water to end the drought... this won't be easy, but it won't be impossible either. The previously listed plans will produce about another 9 trillion gallons of water over the span of four years. This means we only need about another 2.2 trillion gallons of water over 4 years, or about 550 billion gallons of water each year. This can be found in multiple ways, but the most efficient and effective would be cloud seeding. Cloud seeding can increase precipitation and is a true technological and 21st century innovation. It is also very cost effective. The cost to increase precipitation rates effectively where they need to be increased varys. It will cost about $3 Billion to DOUBLE our current annual rainfall and with our rainwater recyclers, this will only give us even more water than the water that is given. This annual cost, along with the others, and along with the plans will effectively and efficiently end our drought within four years.

Chapter 10
Closing Statement

"Give all the power to the many, they will oppress the few. Give all the power to the few, they will oppress the many." -Alexander Hamilton

---

I believe that America has the potential to be so amazing… it is amazing right now but we can make it so much better. We can make breakthroughs in science, we can make our economy so large, we can lower the unemployment rate so low that less than 1% of Americans are unemployed. We can change the tax code so that everyone pays a fair proportional amount and eliminate loopholes so people don't find a way to legally pay no income tax. We can stop being so inefficient with our money. We can finally create a surplus and eliminate our National debt. We can change the healthcare system so that way premiums don't rise upwards of 100% at times. We can change the educational system so that students are invested in and education will become localized rather than federalized. We can fix our crumbling infrastructure so our water will be drinkable in places like Flint and we will be able to drive on our roads and our street lights will work. We can reform the criminal justice system so that people are punished much more fairly. We can fix our system and we can put our nation back to work. We can end disastrous trade deals. We can lower inflation. We can make our military so large that we don't have to use it rather than so small that we can't use it. We can create so much money and stop taxing corporations out of business. We can end illegal immigration and subsidization of illegal immigrants. We can stop allowing hazardous chemicals/ingredients to be put in our food that we give to our children. We, together, can make the future of America free, safe, and prosperous but only with someone who has the stance to lead.

Index

beat, 5

because, 6

become, 5

below, 4

bend, 7

benefits, 8

beyond, 10

biggest, 7

boats, 6

body, 10

book, 2

border, 4

born, 4

both, 5

built, 4

bullet, 5

bullets, 5